THE
TRUTH of LIFE

A Path to Self-Discovery

AHMED HULUSI

As with all my works, this book is not copyrighted.
As long as it remains faithful to the original,
it may be freely printed, reproduced, published and translated.
For the knowledge of ALLAH, there is no recompense.

THE
TRUTH OF LIFE

A Path to Self-Discovery

AHMED HULUSI

www.ahmedhulusi.org/en/

Translated by ALIYA ATALAY

ABOUT THE COVER

The black background of the front cover represents darkness and ignorance, while the white color of the letters represents light and knowledge.

The image is a Kufi calligraphy of the Word of Unity: *"La ilaha illallah; Muhammad Rasulullah"* which means,

"There is no concept such as 'god', there is only that which is denoted by the name Allah, and **Muhammad (SAW)** is the *Rasul* of this understanding."

The placement of the calligraphy, being on top and above everything else on the page, is a symbolic representation of the predominant importance this understanding holds in the author's life.

The green light, reflecting from the window of the Word of Unity, opens up from the darkness into luminosity to illustrate the light of Allah's *Rasul*. This light is embodied in the book's title through the author's pen and concretized as the color white, to depict the enlightenment the author aims to attain in this field. As the knowledge of Allah's *Rasul* disseminates, those who are able to evaluate this knowledge attain enlightenment, which is represented by the white background of the back cover.

CONTENTS

1

MAN, WORLD, UNIVERSE, ISLAM

We live in our cocoon world. Yet we think our cocoon is the real world!

If you were to ask anyone, "Where are you living right now?" they will tell you some place on earth. If you were to say, "So you're from space?" they will say, "Why, of course not. I'm from earth!" But where is earth? Realistically speaking, we are but a speck in the universe, an infinitesimal piece of space. But, due to our age-old conditionings, we would rather believe we live in a fixed world in which the sun and the universe rotate around us, instead of acknowledging our place in the infinite vastness of space! Despite the increasing discoveries of modern science, we are still incognizant of certain Truths!

"We are from earth!" we say.

If you were asked your age, you would reply with a number: thirty, forty, fifty… But is that really your age? To what reference does that number apply?

The earth rotates at a distance of approximately 150 million km around the sun, which is about 1,333,000 times bigger than our earth. When the earth rotates 30 times around the sun we say we are

30 years old. In other words, we mean to say, "Since I was born, the earth has rotated around the sun 30 times." Thus we 'measure' our age.

But in the meantime we overlook or perhaps are completely unaware of a critical fact:

The way we see it, each and every single one of us is existing within our cocoon worlds and we are making inter-cocoon connections among each other. Our communications are based on either the set of values binding our own cocoon or that of another. We are completely oblivious to the reality, the actual dimensions of existence outside of our cocoon world!

Perhaps we don't want to be aware of it..

Perhaps we are afraid... Afraid to think, afraid of becoming confused. Afraid of the unknown, from things we feel we won't be able to comprehend or overcome.

But what are the realities outside our cocoon world?

We are all bound by an undeniable Truth: Our time on earth is limited. At some point, we will all move on. We will all experience what is commonly referred to as death!

There is a point that we must realize:

Just as the earth rotates around the sun, the sun rotates around the center of our galaxy, the Milky Way. So too are our earth and we, together with the sun, rotating around the center of our galaxy. Our sun is about 32 thousand light years away from the center of our galaxy and it takes 255 million years for it complete one rotation. In other words, one year on the sun is the equivalent of 255 million years on earth!

So, a real solar year is actually 255 million earth years! So, if we were to define our age, not in terms of earth years, but in respect to the sun's rotation around the center of the galaxy, then in 255 million years we would have aged by one year!

We currently exist on earth, but at some point, through the experience of death, the earth is going to be lost from our perception. For our perception of earth is based on our five senses – what we see as earth, our world, is only as much as our physical eyes allow us to see and experience! Our sight is limited to a narrow bandwidth of 4,000 to 7,000 Angstroms! All that we see and define as 'existent' are as a result of our brain's interpretation of the intercepted wavelengths within this range. Our hearing range, on the other hand, is only between 16 and 16,000 Hertz. What we perceive as sound is limited to wavelengths within this range. As such, our perception of the world, and our judgment regarding whether something exists or does not exist, is based on these very limited senses. In reality, the scope of existence outside this bandwidth is infinite! Due to our sheer ignorance, we assume all that is outside of our perceptive range to be inexistent.

The earth on which we live is going to fall outside the range of our five-sense perception upon death, and thus become unperceivable to us, but we are going to continue to exist with what is referred to as our spirit, astral or luminous bodies, within the magnetic field of the earth, and subject to the magnetic pull of the sun.[1]

Even though our physical bodily connection will end through death, our spirit-bodies will continue to live within the Von Allen radiation belt subject to the magnetic field of the earth within the platform of the sun, just as we are currently doing so. However, the earth will not be perceivable to us in this new state of existence; we will continue our lives on the radial platform of the sun, only this time with our spirit-perception rather than our bodily sense perception.

---

[1] A detailed explanation of how the spirit-body is produced by the brain has been given in *The Essence of Man, Man Spirit Jinn* and *The Essential Principles of Islam* by Ahmed Hulusi.

So, if the earth disappears from our sight, by which dimension of life will we be bound?

If the concept of earthly time is invalid at this time, but we continue to rotate around the sun, will we be subject to the time zone of the sun? That is, 255 million years will be equivalent to a year by our current viewpoint!

Assuming we live for 70 years on earth, what will this figure mean to us when we die? Since we will be subject to the time zone of the sun, and one year in respect to the sun is 255 million years, then 70 years will be the equivalent of 8.6 seconds. That is, someone who dies at the age of 70 and transits to the next dimension of life – bound by the time zone of the sun – is going to say, "How long did I live on earth? Was my life no longer than a dream?"

In the Quran, this is referred to by the verse, **"The day they see it, it will be as though they had not remained (in the world), except for a time of sunset or twilight."**[2] The original word used for sunset or twilight is *ashiyya*, which is equivalent to the time of the evening prayer. As known, this is the short period of redness in the sky disappearing after sunset. The time when the sun is no longer visible, but its light has not totally disappeared; the brief time only moments before darkness.

When you gaze up at the sky and the redness of the newly set sun disappears, and though you can still see the things around you, suddenly darkness descends... This is how short it's going to feel when a person dies, leaves the time zone of the earth, enters the dimension of the grave and becomes subject to the time zone of the sun!

When we dream during our sleep, based on earthly and physical senses and our current concept of time, our dreams last around 40 to 50 seconds. But, while we are dreaming, those few seconds feel much longer. Nevertheless, when we wake up and think about our dream, we say it was simply a dream... A few brief seconds... Nothing more.

---

[2] Quran 79:46

In the same way, we are told that when we die and move on to the next dimension of existence or the dimension of the sun, looking back on our life at earth we are going to say, "It was as though we remained (in the world), only for a time of sunset or twilight." This is the reality revealed to us in the 49th verse of chapter *an-Naziat* in the Quran. On the other hand, we are also told:

"They will say, 'We remained a day or part of a day; ask those who count.'

He said, 'You remained there only a short while, if only you knew!'"[3]

What does a dream of a few seconds or the time of sunset mean to us the next day?

Death is going to make us 'realize' that our 70-year life span on earth was only 8.6 sun seconds long!

All of our struggles on earth, our griefs, our fights, are all within these few seconds!

And note that this 70-year period is in reference to gross life span! Childhood, youth, old age, senility are all included. So, if we take the net period of conscious evaluation of life, how many seconds remain?

According to Islam, our life on earth is for the sole purpose of preparing for life after death; for constructing our spirit-bodies and developing the resources for our journey of life after death.

Through death we shall 'change dimensions'! And life in that dimension shall last until Doomsday. That is, millions and billions of years! While the time we spend here, in terms of the sun time zone, is a matter of a few seconds!

In fact, we are living on the radial platform of the sun right now, for every form on earth sustains its life from the energy of the sun. In

---

[3] Quran 23:113-114

other words, Allah's attribute of life enlivens and nourishes us via the rays of light that reach our earth from the sun.

So, we come to life on the platform of the sun, we live within the platform of the sun, and we die and change dimensions, again, on the platform of the sun.

The word 'Doomsday' may denote various dimensions and types of transformations, and until the time of Doomsday in the absolute sense, it continually manifests itself as such. However, because of our five-sense limitation, we are unaware of it. For our evaluation of life is obstructed...

So, what should one who lives for 70 years do in this period, which in actuality is equivalent to only 8 seconds or so?

If we have knowledge and insight, we should be cognizant of the fact there are billions of galaxies like the Milky Way in the universe. And the distance between these galaxies cannot be comprehended or perceived by our concepts of measurement. We express these amounts with mathematical figures, but we have no real understanding of what this distance is, for it is beyond human perception.

Forget the billions of other galaxies and the distances between them, our own galaxy alone comprises 400 billions stars – even this is beyond our comprehension!

Right now there about 5 billion[4] humans on planet earth. If we multiply this by ten, taking into consideration all humans that have ever lived on earth throughout the ages, it would be 50 billion people! Yet it has been scientifically confirmed that the Milky Way galaxy constitutes approximately 400 billion stars. So, if we were to send each person to a star in our galaxy we would only be populating 50 billion of these stars. There are 400 billion stars in the Milky Way!

I'm relating this information to give an idea of the galaxy and the vastness of the space in which we live. Now consider how primitive

---

[4] This was written in 1990.

a notion it is to think there is a god outside our galaxy or in the galaxy, say on the constellation Orion or elsewhere! This is the primitive notion Muhammad (saw) tried to eradicate 1,400 years ago! He tried to accentuate the Truth through the Quran, saying, "*La ilaha illaAllah*: There is no god or godhood. There is only Allah!"[5] That is, there is no god out there in space – this concept is invalid – and, as such, doing or offering things for this external god is also an invalid concept. There is no such god awaiting such things. There is only Allah! There is only a single universal Consciousness that has manifested the universe and perhaps even other universes of which we are unaware! It is with this Consciousness, through its knowledge and in its knowledge, that the infinite universes, galaxies and beings have come to life and have become perceivable. Thus, every being can find Allah in their own essence, as everything and everyone is a manifestation of the knowledge and reality of Allah!

There is no god outside and beyond you! Allah has brought everything into existence from His own existence, thus every individual can find and feel Allah in their essence!

This understanding of Allah is the primary pivotal point of Islam! The common message of all Rasuls and Nabis is '*La ilaha illaAllah*'. In fact, the narration that '*La ilaha illaAllah* is written on the gates of Paradise' is in reference to this Truth.

Allah's Nabis and Rasuls have been delegated to inform the people there is no such concept as god, and so all practices done in the name of an external imagined god is useless; there is only Allah! Each of them have offered different recommendations to the people to which they were assigned, depending on their level of understanding and development.

And now for the Truth of life... Let us try to understand the 'system' called 'Islam' created in Allah's knowledge and offered to us as 'religion.'

We, the human species, have emerged on the planet we call earth, within the solar system inside this particular galaxy called the Milky

---

[5] See *Muhammad's Allah* by Ahmed Hulusi for more details.

Way. But we have not made a request to exist, nor were we asked whether we wanted to...

I came to life in the Milky Way, but I was not asked if I wanted to come to life in this particular galaxy... Inside the Milky Way, I came to life in this solar system, but I was not asked if this particular solar system was my preference... I came to life on planet earth, but I was not asked anything about this either... This too was outside my choice and will... I was not asked on which continent I wanted to come to life either! I came to life in Turkey, right in the middle of Asia and Europe, a place called Eurasia. But I wasn't asked where in Turkey I wanted to come to life, nor was I asked of which nationality, gender, religion or community I wanted to be from! I came to life right in the middle of Istanbul, in the Cerrahpasa district! But I wasn't even asked which family I wanted to be born to, or which set of genes I wanted to have! I found myself born of a mother called 'Adalet'! I was blessed with the genes of a sublime family, born as a male, all without my choice! Neither my gender nor any of my physical or intellectual properties were my choice. In short, nothing with which I have been bestowed is a result of my choice or will! I just found myself at this point!

In search of a being to whom I can ask, "Why am I like this?" I lift my head and see the sun, which is 150 million km away and 1,333,000 times bigger than earth... My sight cannot reach it... My comprehension cannot grasp its enormity! And then I'm told there are 400 billion other stars just like the sun in our galaxy alone... To whom shall I turn in this infinite vastness; to whom shall I ask "Why" and "How"?... I cannot find anyone! I'm left with myself, and I have no choice but to accept myself the way I am. Then I say to myself, "Let me try to understand this system in which I have been born, to the best of my bodily and intellectual capability." There is nothing I can do to change the past. The only thing I can do at this point is understand the kind of future awaiting me and hence live my life accordingly – to use my choice at least after this point, to prepare for a future in which I can be peaceful and happy.

When I look at the Truth of life, this is what I see: I exist in a world, of whose actual reality I am unaware... And at a time unknown to me, I'm going to part from this world... But will I become inexistent? Since nothing that 'exists' will become 'inexistent' and everything that exists undergoes some form of transformation and continues its life in a new dimension and under new conditions of life, I know, based on this logic, that my consciousness too will undergo a transformation and I will continue my life in a new state of existence under new conditions of life.

They call this death...

Death... An experience awaiting each and every single one of us...

According to the Quran, death is an event 'to be tasted':

"Every individual consciousness will taste death (life without a biological body will continue eternally)."[6]

Therefore, after having tasted death, 'I' will continue to live... To put it another way, I will continue my life without the biological body, as my connection to this body is going to be severed. However, because I have been identifying with this body my entire life and uploading data to my consciousness as if I were no more than this body, when this connection is severed, it will feel as though I am being buried alive, I'm going to feel fully conscious, aware and alive when they bury me! They're going to put me under the ground and cover me with soil, and I'm going to watch and feel all of this ... Then I will be transferred to the realm of the grave... This is the event to which the Quran refers as the 'tasting of death'!

The Rasul of Allah (saw) told Omar (ra) about how a person continues to see the people around him during burial and hear their calling after being placed into the grave, "O Omar, you will continue your life in the grave with the same consciousness and comprehension as the consciousness and comprehension you have here today!" And he calls out to the graves of those who died in the Battle of Badr, and when those who think they are dead say, "Why are you talking to the dead, can they hear you, O Rasulullah?" He

---

[6] Quran 3:185

answers, "Indeed... They hear and understand me better than the way you do and they confirm what I say!"

So, do not think of those who have been buried as dead; they are alive and conscious! Yet, because their bodies are no longer in use, they are unable to contact us by means of their physical bodies. But they have full perception of us. It is for this reason that it is useful to console someone who has just passed away.

Death is the gateway to a new dimension of life! And in this new dimension of life we will have a new astral or wave body, which in religious terms has been referenced as 'the spirit.' But the most crucial point is that we are continually and simultaneously building our spirit-bodies in this world by and through our current biological brain! That is why it has been said in a hadith, "The world is the sowing field of the hereafter; what you sow here you will reap in the hereafter." That is, the body that you generate and build here, you will use there! You will have no excuse to complain about your body there, for you will have designed and built it yourself with your brain in this world!

When we get to the platform of the afterlife, the platform of the sun, each of us is going to see this Truth and say, "I wish I could return to the world and do the things I neglected, and have the opportunity to build a new spirit-body so we don't have to put up with the distress here!"

The Quran says:

"When death comes to one of them, he says, 'My Rabb, send me back (to the worldly life). So that I might do righteousness in that which I left behind (i.e. a faithful life that I did not heed or give importance to; the potential that I did not utilize and activate).' No! (It is impossible to go back!) His words are invalid! (His request is unrecognized in the system) and behind them is a barrier (an isthmus; a difference of dimension) until the Day they are resurrected (they cannot go back;

reincarnation, being re-born for another worldly life, is not possible!)."[7]

According to the Quran and the Rasul of Allah, reincarnation, or coming back to this world in another form and having another chance at fulfilling certain practices, is absolutely not possible! We will be bound by whatever we did in the world. But what is our real chance at attaining this eternal life to come while in this world?

According to our understanding, 20 years, 30 years, or perhaps 50 or 60 years… But all of this only accounts for a few seconds in terms of the platform of the sun.

So, we only really have a few seconds to attain a state of life that will last for millions and billions of years. Either we are going to try and understand this and live our lives accordingly or give no importance to this Truth and face its bitter consequence for billions of years.

Please let me reiterate, there is no god up in the heavens who is going to send you to his paradise for dressing in a particular way or to his hell for enraging him! Discern this well! There is only Allah, the creator of the multiple universes! And many scientists and religious figures are unaware of the difference between the god concept and the reality denoted by the name Allah! The choice is ours! We may not have had any choice in anything up to this point in our lives, but from this point on we are face to face with using our choice consciously. So, we must either cleanse ourselves from all our past conditionings and the beliefs we acquired from our environment and genuinely inquire the Truth, or completely put aside thought and be willing to face its harsh consequences!

We must understand the reality of death and what we must do to adequately prepare for the life awaiting us after it. Based on this, Muhammad (saw) has recommended certain practices in light of the Truths that were revealed to him. The foundation of these practices is the magnificent system and order of which we are a part, it is in complete compliance with the mechanism of life – not to please a

---

[7] Quran 23:99-100

god out there! The Rasul of Allah (saw) informs us of the system in which we are living and its conditions so that we may comprehend and prepare for our future, lest we are faced with severe consequences. The practices advised by Rasulullah (saw) to which we refer as 'worship' or 'prayer' are not directed to an external deity-god, it is purely to equip and prepare us for a favorable future life, based on the mechanisms of the 'system'.

We can either take his recommendations seriously and prudently prepare for our future, or ignore and dismiss the Truth he has shown us at our own expense.

For all the practices advised by the Rasul of Allah (saw) are the very things that are necessary for the things we are to encounter. Religion is the system, and the name of this system is Islam. None can alter it, add to it or reduce from it in anyway. The Rasul of Allah (saw) has informed us of this system based on divine revelation. He had the authority to talk on behalf of Allah, but this authority has been taken from mankind since his departure to the next dimension.

Personal religious opinions (*fatwa*) do not bind anyone! Everyone, from Hadhrat Abu Bakr (ra) and Hadhrat Ali (ra) to an individual today, has the right to express their views and understanding of religion. But nobody has the jurisdiction to talk on behalf of the religion, Allah or the Quran. Thus, the only authority binding all of us is Muhammad (saw).

Muhammad (saw) informed everyone, including all future generations, 1,400 years ago of the things we need to do. The responsibility of each individual lies with himself. Being subject to another will in no way relieve the individual from his responsibilities.

AHMED HULUSI

Antalya, 1990

2

KNOW YOUR SELF – DISCOVER YOUR ESSENTIAL REALITY

The foundation of all knowledge is based on knowing Allah. The knowledge of one who does not know Allah is meaningless.

"They did not justly appraise (the manifestations of the qualities denoted by the Name) Allah." [8]

"Did you see the one who deified his baseless desires and thus who Allah led astray in line with his knowledge (assumption) and sealed his ability to sense the reality and veiled his vision?"[9]

"Do not turn to (assume the existence of) a god (exterior manifestations of power or your illusory self) besides Allah."[10]

---

[8] Quran 22:74
[9] Quran 45:23
[10] Quran 28:88

"Say: 'Allah' and let them amuse themselves in their empty discourse (their illusory world) in which they are absorbed."[11]

Evident is the Truth if only you wished to see... It is the Self that exists, if only you can erase your name! You think you exist, yet this is only your assumption! The Truth is your essence, if only you can see your 'self'!

I named one of my books *Muhammad's Allah*. Some may find it a little striking. They may wonder, "Why not name it just *Allah*, why *Muhammad's Allah*?" Simply because the majority of the people use this name to reference their own imagined gods! What they reference as 'Allah' in their heads has nothing to do with the reality of Allah at all. Unfortunately, the majority of these people, who base their lives around their postulated deity-gods, are going to end up in severe loss and disappointment when they find out such gods do not exist.

In *Muhammad's Allah* I tried to explain how and why Allah is not a 'god' in the general sense, and that traditional conceptions of god, based on age-old conditionings, have nothing to do with the reality disclosed by Muhammad (saw).

Everyone, from the least developed to the most developed, has an understanding of a god... A deity who they love and respect, or get angry with from time to time... As if He is a benevolent father sitting on a star or a majestic sultan in the heavens – while those with broader views claim such a god cannot exist and declare not to be believers.

It is important to understand that the practices recommended by the Rasul of Allah (saw) are the very things that are going to be necessary for a person in his life after death in order to live in bliss and not be subject to harm. Whether the person takes advantage of these recommendations or not, its consequences binds him alone.

Hence the Quran says, "**There is no compulsion in** (acceptance of) **the religion** (the system and order of Allah; sunnatullah)"[12] That is, no individual or organization or government has the right or

---

[11] Quran 6:91
[12] Quran 2:256

responsibility to enforce a religious regulation upon another person, as this isn't something that can be achieved via compulsion. Say you are a believer, but you do not attend the congregational Friday prayer, but you believe in Allah, the authenticity of the Quran and that Muhammad (saw) is the Rasul of Allah... Now, if I were to threaten and force you into attending the Friday prayers, you may end up going, but totally unwillingly. Doing something without really wanting to is a form of hypocrisy! Hence, through compulsion, a believer is reduced to the state of a hypocrite! Nobody has the right to enforce such a reduction upon anyone! None has the jurisdiction to impose a religious law upon anyone! This is what the Quran teaches; the Quran encourages everyone to draw their paths according to their own conscious will and reason.

Hence, it is said Islam is an 'invitation'!

The practices known as the pillars of Islam are 'offers'; they give the person the option of either complying with certain recommendations to reach favorable outcomes or refusing to do so at their own expense. It is the choice of the person whether they want to take advantage of this or not.

Islam encourages the person to take up certain practices as a result of their own conscious choice based on their own personal belief and in preparation of their own hereafter. There is no compulsion! Besides, all of us are invited to follow the Rasul of Allah (saw), not a *sheikh* or a *tariqah* or any particular school of Islam. Religion addresses the intellect; it encourages contemplation and inquisition. Religion encourages the individual to draw and direct their own path in life. Therefore, each person's understanding of the Quran and the teachings of Rasulullah (saw) is to themselves. Islam does not stipulate any form of blind following! On the contrary, it encourages man to use his intellect and reason.

This is why I stress the importance of research and inquiry to define the direction of one's life. This is why I refrain from imposing a religious leadership role upon anyone and do not call anyone to follow my understanding or me! Regardless of how the ignorant ones want to label me, these labels have no validity. Religious labels, ranks and positions are inapplicable in Islam.

We must evaluate the teachings of religion realistically. The practices that are advised by the Rasul of Allah (saw) are not a 'package deal.' It's not like you have to do either all or none. This is an erroneous view. The Quran advises many practices, such as performing *salat*, fasting, giving alms (*zakah*), performing the pilgrimage (hajj), abstaining from things like lying, rumors, adultery and gambling, etc… The extent to which we apply these in our lives is how much we will benefit, and the extent to which we neglect them will define the consequences we will face. If one can fast during Ramadan, but not perform the daily *salat* that is fine; it would be wrong to abandon fasting just because one does not pray. It is an enormous mistake to make such claims and stop people from praying or fasting. The consequences of not fulfilling certain practices binds that person alone; none has the right to make judgments on behalf of Allah!

Unfortunately, many concepts of Islam are misunderstood today. One very important topic is regarding the headscarf. While the consequences of not fulfilling certain practices, such as praying and fasting, have been clearly explained by Rasulullah (saw), no such claim has been made regarding women who do not wear a scarf. It is unfortunate that religion is reduced to dress code and appearance, and in the case of women, to wearing a scarf. Some even go as far as claiming women who do not wear a scarf are considered unbelievers. According to my understanding, this is a very incorrect viewpoint. There is not a single verse or hadith about what will happen to a woman if she does not wear a scarf! Therefore, none has the right to make any judgment about what she may face if a woman chooses not to wear it. We may only say, "This is something between her Rabb and herself – the judgment belongs to Allah alone."

Having said this, nothing can be a greater mistake than her saying, "Since I do not wear a scarf, I might as well not pray either"! If she chooses not to wear a scarf, that is fine. She can still pray, fast and perform pilgrimage. Just as she wears a scarf during prayer then takes it off during her daily life, she may perform pilgrimage with the necessary dress code, then continue her life with her usual clothing afterwards. Her choice not to wear a scarf is between Allah and herself, but it is not in any way preventing her performance of pilgrimage.

This is how everyone should evaluate their lives! In terms of the time zone that is of relevance to us, we are only living a few seconds of life on earth. The Rasul of Allah (saw) says, "People are asleep; upon death they will awaken." They will wake up with death! The implications of this statement looks to both physical reality and consciousness. It is in this dream-like life we are currently living that we have the opportunity to prepare for the eternal life awaiting us after death. But most of our lives pass us by without our realizing the Truth – with the hustle and bustle of childhood, youth, adulthood and career years, etc. We don't even know how much longer we have, perhaps we have already neared the end of our lives! A sudden car accident may be it! The point of no return!

So, let us use this short time wisely! It is like our house has caught fire and we have only seconds to save whatever we can! Whatever has burnt has burnt and we don't have time to mourn over the past; we must only concentrate on what we can do from this point on. To claim, "But I do not wear a scarf," and neglect all the other practices, is the greatest mistake one can make! Let everyone look to the things they 'can' do! Let the ones who can attend the Friday prayer, attend the Friday prayer, and the ones who can pray 23 times a day, pray 23 times a day!

Good for those who can pray five times a day, but to say I can't pray five times so I might as well not pray at all is plain absurdity. If you can't pray five times then pray four times, if not four then three. Even if you just pray your morning prayer before you leave the house, it is better than not praying at all.

To do something is better than doing nothing at all!

If you go to work and say, "Today I aim to make ten thousand dollars," but you only make two, do you refuse the two because you didn't reach your goal? Of course not! Whatever you make is a profit! The same goes for the life of the world; whether you're a male or a female, young or old, the past is past and we do not have time to wail over the past! A long unknown path lies ahead of us, we must look to make the best of this journey, whatever we can do will be for our benefit. A little profit is better than loss. This is the principle of religious practices, for we are not going to have the opportunity to come back to fix or do more.

Consider this: What we eat is converted into energy for our body, which forms the bioelectrical energy in microvolts needed by brain cells. The brain then generates a specific wave of energy with this power. This wave forms the spirit-body and our brain capacity – knowledge, comprehension and what we call 'spirit strength', our spiritual potential, is uploaded to our spirit-body by the brain. The point at which the brain stops functioning, we continue our lives within the platform of the sun with the consciousness formed by all the data that has been uploaded to our spirit-body throughout our lives. This phase, bound to the magnetic field of the earth, will last until Doomsday and it has been referred to as the realm of the grave or *barzah*. One who makes this transition can never return to the world or have the chance to upload new data with a new brain ever again! This is why it is imperative for us to adequately prepare for our future life while we have the chance.

Now, I want to touch on a very simple topic. We make ablution before we pray. If we were to inquire into its necessity, we will most probably be told it is for cleansing and purification. Whereas, there were times when the Rasul of Allah (saw) made ablution with a glass of water. Today, in most Middle Eastern countries in hot climates ablution is made with a small cup of water. Especially if we take into consideration *tayammum* – rubbing dirt on our face in the absence of water – it becomes evident that ablution is not about cleansing! Not in the general sense, anyway. Then, why take ablution? What is it about? Just as the body absorbs air through osmosis, it also absorbs water. That is, when water makes contact with our skin, energy through water molecules is transmitted to the nervous system via osmosis. As for *tayammum*, static energy that exerts pressure and stress on the brain is neutralized through soil. As such, all practices of worship are based on scientific, physical and chemical laws of the system in which we are living.

The Absolute Existence referenced as 'Allah' in the Quran, the creator of the universe, has created everything with the qualities of His Names. That is, all the qualities and attributes with which we have been endowed derive from those divine qualities. Man has been declared the vicegerent of earth because he contains within his essence all of the 99 Names of Allah.

"And when your Rabb said to the angels (personifications of the qualities of the Names comprising one's body, hence the addressee here is you), 'I will make upon the earth (the body) a vicegerent (conscious beings who will live with the awareness of the Names)'..."[13]

"We have made you a vicegerent on earth!"[14]

Note that the verses in regards to man's vicegerency are in reference to humans in general without denoting a gender difference. Men and women are equal in the sight of Allah in terms of their vicegerency potential. None can claim women are second to men. The vicegerency potential is equally inherent in both.

Now, let us take a deeper look. Since we have all come to life with the Names of Allah, just as the Names such as *Rahman*, *Rahim*, *Murid*, *Malik* and *Quddus* are present within all of us, we also contain the divine attributes pertaining to Allah's Absolute essence. For example, the *Hayy* (life) attribute of Allah is present within us, thus we are alive. Allah's attribute of knowledge is present within us, thus we are conscious beings. Similarly, the quality of will denoted by the Name *Murid* is present within us, thus we will things, and with the quality of power, *Qadir*, we have the power to actualize the things we will. In short, we exist with the qualities and attributes comprising the Names of Allah.

We have not been informed of these Names in the Quran to be introduced to a deity-god out there, but so we may know our true selves, our essential reality.

"One who knows himself, knows his Rabb." (Hadith)

---

[13] Quran 2:30
[14] Quran 38:26

The extent to which you know your self – the qualities and attributes comprising your being – is the extent to which you will know Allah, the essence and reality of existence. But no matter how well you know Allah in this respect, you can never truly know or comprehend Him in terms of His Absolute Essence (*dhat*). For, it is not possible for our limited cognition to discern the infiniteness of His Absolute Essence.

So, if we have all come to be with His Being – the qualities of His Names – we are all manifestations of His constitutional qualities and attributes, and thus, as His vicegerents, we all deserve love and respect! No matter what our name, color, race, language or religion may be, we must show love and respect to each other! For the being beneath that name, color, race, language and religion belongs to Allah! The person from whom you turn away, hate, dislike or look down upon is also the manifestation of Allah's Names and qualities!

Prostration is not just about placing your forehead on the floor, it is to understand that everything in existence is the existence of Him alone; all forms pertain to His countenance, He is not separate from existence! If we can come to this discernment we will no longer be able to discriminate among creation. We will only see 'humans' – the 'vicegerents' of Allah on earth. Regardless of their race, color, religion or culture, what is incumbent upon us is to show utmost love and respect to all forms of life.

We will pass through this world conditioned and blind to Allah and the Truths and suffer eternally as a result. Failing to recognize one's own reality leads automatically to not being able to recognize the reality of others, and thus, being stuck in one's cocoon world.

We must either become a butterfly and break through the cocoon or fail to develop and, like the silkworm, be cast into fire inside the silk! To be in the silk and be cast into boiling water must not be a nice experience!

So, O you covered in silk! Become a butterfly, break your cocoon and fly… Pull yourself together and recognize the Truth. Listen to the call of Rasulullah (saw) and try to evaluate his teachings. Salvage your eternal life! Everything you are asked to do is for your own sake. Neither Allah needs you, or the Rasul of Allah, or the Quran! It is for your own future that you must take heed of these words! For your remorse later will never be of benefit to you!

There are about 5 billion[15] people on earth today. If we were to gather these 5 billion people together, the chances of you finding someone you know among them is one in 5 billion. When you die, you're going to leave this world and go the realm of the grave and live there for millions of years, and then everyone is going to be gathered during Doomsday. I wonder how many of the people you love and value today will you be able to find at that point...?

When we die and our connection to this body is severed, we will be placed into the grave in a conscious state. We will see and hear everything, all the insects and bugs in the grave, the people outside, but we will not be able to leave the grave. Just like the things we do and think about during the day enters our dream at night, but we have no control over it in the dream state. Based on "the people in the world are asleep, upon death they will awaken" the consequences of everything you live and identify with in the worldly life will become apparent in the realm of the grave.

After some time, as the material-physical world disappears from the person's perception, the physical aspect of the grave will also disappear and the person will begin to live in the dimension of the spirit. This means the world will totally disappear and the person will commence his life within the platform of the sun. Consequently, he will begin to perceive all the entities and life forms in the sun and other parts of the galaxy. This is why it has been said a window will be opened to the person in the grave through which he will gaze upon hell and heaven. Distance does not apply to the eye of the spirit.

While our physical eye can only see up to 50, 100 or 1,000 meters, the concept of distance is totally invalid for the eye of the spirit – it can perceive a place 150 million km away as if it is only at a distance of a few meters.

---

[15] This was written in 1990.

According to one scientific view, a body that weighs 70kg on earth will weigh 300,000kg on the sun. Interestingly, there are hadiths in regards to the enormity of the bodies of those who will go to hell.

A person who enters the grave will then begin to perceive the sun and the forms of life therein. If they are to remain in hell eternally, they will see heaven, the life they will miss out on, and the suffering awaiting them in hell, which will cause them suffering in their grave, just like seeing a nightmare.

On the other hand, a person who is to enter paradise will be filled with joy and tranquility, and this will continue until Doomsday.

The spirit of those who have parted from the world are currently within the magnetic field called Von Allen. The realm of the grave (*barzah*) is the magnetic life inside this belt.

When the sun expands and engulfs and evaporates Mercury, Venus and the earth, the earth will totally disappear. According to my understanding, Doomsday entails the expansion of the sun and its engulfment of the earth, after which the Von Allen belt and the magnetic field of the earth will also cease to exist.

After this, everyone will be gathered within the magnetic field of the sun and everyone will have the opportunity to evaluate their life on earth, what they've done, what they've failed to do, etc. That is, all symbolic expressions pertaining to 'the Place of Gathering' or *mahshar* will transpire. After this, those who have fulfilled certain requisites will be removed from this state of hell and progress to another dimension of life, commonly referred to as heaven.

The rest will remain in the magnetic field of the sun. That the sun is hell is my own construal. But the fact the sun is growing and is to reach a point of engulfing the earth is based completely on scientific data.

This being the case, what should we do?

Since we are simultaneously forming our spirit-body during our life on earth through our brain, we must optimize the use of our brain

– use its potential to the extent that we can. For example, they say people only use about 5% to 7% of their brain capacity while the rest is in an inert state. This leads us to the introduction of another important topic: *dhikr* – the repetition of certain words, prayers and Names of Allah.

Why do we engage in *dhikr*? What are its effects?

Dhikr is the most important thing a person can do! As stated above, *dhikr* is not to invoke a god out there, for the very qualities of Allah are the qualities with which we have been formed and created. The qualities such as *Rahman, Rahim, Murid, Quddus* and *Fattah* are all present within us! How so? Obviously not as words or shapes… Every meaning is stored as a vibration of a specific frequency in the brain. Brain cells are in a constant state of electrical vibration. Every thought stimulates a vibration and an electrical influx among specific clusters of cells in the brain.

In 1986 I wrote about how *dhikr*, the repetition of specific words, stimulates a specific electrical reaction in the brain, activating the inert cells through transmitters and programming them to the frequency of the repeated word, thus activating the inactive areas of the brain and expanding its capacity.

Seven years after I wrote this, *Scientific American*[16] made its first report in regards to this topic, claiming certain cells in the brain are activated via the repetition of specific words leading to an increase of brain capacity.

What I'm trying to say in short is, you can expand the capacity of your brain, through the practice of *dhikr*, in line with the meaning of the Name you repeat. So, for example, the name *Murid* is the third of the Seven Essential Attributes of Allah and it is in reference to Divine Will. If you repeat this name a few thousand times every day, you will witness an observable difference in the strength of your willpower within a few weeks or months. Alongside *Murid*, if you also repeat *Quddus*, you will see a cleansing taking place in your life – a purification from certain addictions, the realization that you are

---

[16] John Horgan, "Fractured Functions," *Scientific American*, December 1993, Volume 269, No 6.

more than your body; an eternal being made to live an infinite life after death, and so on…

Every name has a different effect and increases specific capacities within the brain. The greater a specific capacity in your brain, the more the meaning of that particular Name will become manifest in your life, and based on this, the more you will get to know Allah in line with that meaning. That is to say, the more you realize these qualities within your self, the more you will get to know Allah.

If we stop observing things from an external view and try to see things in terms of self-development we will understand that prayer and *dhikr* are means to increase the capacity of the brain and achieve personal development. And since these are automatically uploaded to the spirit via the brain, the spirit-body will effectively be highly capacitated.

In line with this, other practices such as *salat*, fasting, hajj, etc., also serve the same purpose – to efficiently prepare and equip us for our life to come.

The choice is ours. We can either make use of these tools to build our spirit-bodies and secure our future lives or neglect them at our own expense. We can either understand the reality 'Allah' actually references and shape our lives accordingly, or think of Him as a deity-god out there, who 'does not need our worship', and thus face the bitter consequences at the end.

I have attempted to share the Truths of life with you. I don't know whether it will be of benefit or not, but whether you agree with me or you don't, I urge you to do your own research and validate everything for yourself.

Don't gamble with your life – your eternal life.

Remember, we are only here for a few seconds! The clock is ticking… Make the best of your remaining time. There is no return to this world, according to the Quran! Muhammad (saw) tells us it is not possible for anyone to come back and have a second chance at worldly life. We will not be able to come back and do the things we fail to do now or compensate for our mistakes. None of our current values are going to be applicable in the next dimension of life. So please, be realistic, and live your life in a way that will not cause regret at the end.

May Allah enable us all to live lives that we won't later regret, and allow and simplify for us all an accurate evaluation of the Truths of life!

Stay well, my friends.

AHMED HULUSI

Antalya

3

WHY THE AWAITED GOLDEN AGE IS 'NOW'

The primary and most essential message of the Quran asserted some 1,400 years ago is the reality that the One referenced as **Allah** is the Absolute Oneness other than which nothing exists. This is so by way of his qualities *al-Wahid*, *al-Ahad* and *as-Samad*. In the last 35 years or so science has also been affirming the endless, limitless Oneness of existence. Thus, the awaited '**Golden Age**' is now! What makes it '**golden**' is the emanation of the knowledge of **Oneness** through people. **What is considered a scientific reality today was miraculously disclosed by the Quran over 1,400 years ago**.

Just like smoking has lost its throne in the USA and European countries after its harms have been exposed, but desperately tries to continue its sovereignty in countries that are behind in scientific discoveries, 'materialism' is also completely impoverished in the world of science and serves only as a topic where 'matter' based religious or philosophical debates are concerned in underdeveloped circles.

After discovering '*matter*' to be only a perceptional illusion, physics and medicine have now turned their focus on the brain – as I emphasized in 1985. For the unexposed mysteries are not in the seemingly external world, but within the dimensional depths of the brain that perceives the world. The extent to which the brain, the compositional structure comprising the qualities of the Names of Allah, is explored and its depths are discovered is the nearness to which man may reach his essential reality (Rabb).

Contemporary physics has now entered the theoretical-physics phase and has come face to face with the reality that man, the brain and existence as a whole are formed from a universal energy – that it is waves of data. In other words, we have come to the realization that we live in a holographic universe.

Atheism, sourced from the dualistic materialistic notion of a god *separate from the individual*, has now become scientifically impossible! It has lost its foundations. After the realization that existence is ONE, it is evident that this dualistic outlook is rendered completely obsolete. The final chapter of the Quran, al-Ikhlas, explains this very reality, for those who contemplate!

As the notion of '*matter*' is invalidated; the '*matter-spirit*' duality is depleted. There is no longer a god to be denied. The only observable reality is a singular existence. **Scientific discoveries have ended the dualistic understanding of, "*There is me, and there is also a God far and beyond me*"**!

Atheism essentially spawned from scientists who were indoctrinated with the religious teaching of '*the fatherly god in the heavens and the son*'. Realizing – in the face of the billions of galaxies constituting space – the absurdity and thus the impossibility of a localized physical god who sent his son to earth, these minds have denied the concept of godhood altogether and chosen atheism in opposition to the church. And the church has outcast and cursed them! While these scientists have recognized the reality that there is no god, "La ilaha", they have failed to reach the knowledge contained in the Quran disclosed by **Muhammad** (saw) and thus the knowledge of "**Allah**".

But what if one who is aware of the Oneness of existence fails to accept the teachings of Muhammad (saw) and the Quran? What will they lose? We must delve further into this matter for many people are misled here, thinking the knowledge of Oneness is sufficient.

In the guise of an offering, the Quran is actually a confirmation. Understanding Oneness is a tool for man, not the final objective!

Becoming cognizant of Oneness should yield the following:

1. The person realizes there is no god above or beyond and he is in servitude to the One alone.

2. He recognizes the absolute system and order (Islam) of this Oneness (Allah), and understands that, whatever becomes manifest from him in a previous state, defines what will manifest from him in a later state.

3. Thus, he tries his best to do whatever he can to use the qualities of the Names of Allah in his essence and form his world accordingly.

If, through the realization of Oneness, one is not able to view the 'many from the One,' then Oneness has not yet been fully grasped and experienced, it is only an intellectual understanding, not one that is felt and lived. To view the 'One from the many' will never allow all the answers to be perceived.

The Sufi masters, from Rumi, to Naqshibandi, al-Ghazali, Jilani, Yunus and Bektashi, never contented themselves with the recognition of Oneness, but rather *lived* every moment of their lives by this reality. Thus, they were free from the things that caused them suffering and reached a state of eternal bliss.

Therefore, recognizing and experiencing the **One** is the only **way out**, and the clearest path that leads to this door is to abandon the world of symbols and metaphors, and to make use of our current world of science. Scientific discoveries are the greatest **provision** that the One denoted by 'Allah' manifests through the one denoted by 'man.' This **provision** that has been bestowed upon the conscious ones is the nourishment of the brains forming the '**Golden Age**.'

Science has attained some very important findings:

a. Data that reaches the brain as waves is processed by the brain and each individual experiences its result in **his own holographic world**[17].

b. *'Matter'* has only a RELATIVE existence, based on the perceiver. All perceivers are actually interacting with the data that enters their perception (depending on their capacity) from among the waves of data comprising the universe. It is impossible to perceive the universe in the absolute sense.

c. The essence of *'matter'* has been questioned and it has been found it does not have a separate existence; the universe in **its totality is a SINGLE field of energy (the manifestation of power) and an endless ocean of data waves** in which everything is a hologram.

Let us expand on these a little.

Doubtless, everything we perceive and have an opinion on is merely an *interpretation*. Various data waves that reach our brain via organs, which in turn are also essentially clusters of data waves, are processed and *interpreted* by the brain to form an 'opinion'!

The cluster of data waves/energy, which we call the brain, forms an identity (the ego) based on the information it synthesizes and thus continues its existence in its holographic world eternally.

Man (individual forms of consciousness) is the totality of all this data and continues his life with what manifests through him from his origin – the potential and knowledge of the eternal limitless One – like all other individuals. Though there is only the One, *different perceptions* yield the notion there are many.

Consciousness (man) is immortal, because his origin is immortal! **Man** is knowledge (the composition of the Names of Allah/Spirit)! The body/animal, on the other hand, is depleted and recycled!

---

[17] See *The Observing One* by Ahmed Hulusi, chapter 2, *The Holographic Universe Of Your Mind* for more details.

So, consciousness in the form of 'man' will part from his vehicle of perception, the body, through death (the tasting of life without a body) and continue his existence in a dimension with a different perception.

Consciousness (in the form of man) is a spirit comprised of the Spirit (the qualities of the Names) of Allah. The body, on the other hand, is its vehicle, formed according to the conditions of the worldly life or the tool/organs to perceive the dimension in which it resides.

Thus far we have addressed the micro aspect. As for the macro aspect...

What certain less developed communities do not realize is that we live in a universe made of billions of galaxies, that is, billions that we have discovered so far! All of our knowledge constitutes only 4% of the universal energy... The remaining 96%, according to today's science, is still 'dark'!

Furthermore, if we can realize that *time* and *space* are relative concepts based on the *'perceiver'* and the *'perceived'* and that, in respect of the reality of existence, they mean nothing, we will see that all of our philosophical and religious debates become invalidated and meaningless! It is evident that, in light of scientific authenticity, there is no director-god above or beyond who out of his mercy sent His son to save humanity! In a sense, the sun has risen from the west; scientific discoveries are leading humanity towards the reality of "illaAllah" (there is only Allah)!

This is why I say we have entered the Golden Age in the last 34 years – since the beginning of the Hijri century.

The reason I say the Golden Age is because...

The truth asserted by the Quran, that, **"There is no god or godhood, only Allah – La ilaha illaAllah"**[18] has become undeniably evident through modern science. A material world/universe has become completely obsolete and the reality that

---

[18] See *Muhammad's Allah* by Ahmed Hulusi for more details.

"only Allah exists" has been revealed – even though the majority of the population may not yet be aware of it, thinking they live in a material world of flesh-bone and earth.

Many of the metaphors used in the Quran, or by Muhammad (saw), Moses (s) and Jesus (s), have now been decoded and the mechanisms to which they point have been deciphered. For example, the word 'heaven' (*sama*) denotes both space and the depths of one's existence. The word 'disclosure' (*nuzul/inzal*) means a revealment or an exposal from one's origin Self (*Rububiyyah*) to his field of awareness.

Nevertheless, our knowledge is only as much as Allah allows us to know; as much as the One discloses His knowledge through us – just like the hand can only move with the command and will of the brain.

The Quran accentuates two primary truths:

a. There is only the One denoted by the name **Allah**; nothing exists other than **Him**!

b. Man has been created to manifest the qualities comprising his brain (*Rabb*). To reiterate, one's Rabb is the composition of the Names of Allah comprising his being, not a god up in the heavens. If your Rabb wills it, you may find and get to know Him within yourself!

Using different words, theoretical physics and medicine also affirm the same truths:

The universe, as we know it, is an entire field of data waves. All formations in the universe and everything we perceive from our environment become manifest through the decoding of data waves by what we call the 'brain'. No perceptual or conceptual limitation, including time and space can be applied to this infinite ONEness. The brain/individual consciousness lives in its own world formed according to the knowledge/capacity with which it has been endowed, based on how much the perception organs can perceive. Multiple universes exist only according to the perceivers. In reality there is only the ONE!

The absolute reality (the absolute essence of the One referenced as Allah) can never be known!

The data waves constituting the essence of the multiple universes are actually the non-dual potential designating the totality of Allah's Names, as mentioned in the Quran. All things transpire (or have transpired) in this dimension – the knowledge of Allah.

'**Man**' is essentially a bodiless/formless consciousness composed of divine qualities to observe and/or direct the data that enters his perception according to his data make up. Once again, under the guise of 'man' is the composition of Allah's Names referred to as 'Rabb'.

If we can grasp and comprehend this ONEness and non-duality, we will see that...

While the One referenced as 'Allah' in the Quran creates the multiple universes in His knowledge with His knowledge and lives (*al-Hayy*) this observation in a single instance (now), He is at the same time beyond everything that appears in His observation in terms of His Absolute Essence (*dhat*)!

While He is everything – all of the divine qualities that have become manifest as the multiple universes (*Zahir*) – He reforms and re-manifests Himself anew at every instance. However, He is far beyond being limited by His manifestations (*Batin*).

The extent to which 'man' can decode the metaphors and symbols used in the Quran is the extent to which he can recognize and acknowledge the reality and thus make use of this 'Golden Age.' Only then can he truly appreciate the miraculousness of the knowledge contained in the Quran. And only then can he truly understand that Islam is not about submitting to Allah, but about experiencing the bliss of knowing he is by default in a state of submission to the One whose name is Allah.

There is much more to this topic, but it is not possible to address it all here. It will probably take years to comprehend the things I write; I will probably not see the results. But what matters is that, at some point, somebody will confirm what I am saying. In 1985 I wrote the inevitable end of the planet Earth was to be engulfed by the growing Sun. Today, this fact is being taught in schools in the West, yet Muslims around the world are still in denial. So, it is unrealistic for me to expect the majority to understand and accept the things I'm writing today and hence no need to go into any further detail.

The only other note I can make at this stage is, just like in our current experience of life, we feel and live in what seems to be a material/tangible world – even though we know everything is energy and waves of intangible data – our experience of all other dimensions of life after this world will also be the same – at least for the great majority of us... Only the depths of the perception of those, in the words of Sufism, 'whose veils have been lifted while living in this dimension' will be different. And that is something none has the liberty to talk about other than the one who experiences it.

Let it be known... **This is the generation of the Golden Age. The information contained in the Quran is being scientifically verified and authenticated. Even if it is being done so using different words, terms and expressions!**

The Rasul of Allah (saw) is Truth; all his teachings are the universal reality. Everything the Quran and the Rasul of Allah (saw) says about the mechanism of giving account, which will be activated through death, the hell or heaven-like experiences in the dimension of the grave, the period at the place of gathering (*mahshar*) and all that is to transpire therein, and the final states of life in the dimensions referred to as either heaven or hell are all authentic Truths. I have explained the hows and whys of all of these in many of my books.

Everything disclosed in the Quran is the Truth! For those who are able to READ it!

Note: If this knowledge has not made you forego and sacrifice your '**ego/identity**,' wave goodbye to another Eid void of sacrifice. If **pilgrimage** is made through knowledge and the **One** is attained intellectually, then the sacrifice of the **ego**, the illusory self, has not been actualized!

Blessed be your Eid of Hajj, in this Hijri year of 1434.

AHMED HULUSI

11 October 2013

Raleigh, NC, USA

ABOUT THE AUTHOR

Ahmed Hulusi (Born January 21, 1945, Istanbul, Turkey) contemporary Islamic philosopher. From 1965 to this day he has written close to 30 books. His books are written based on Sufi wisdom and explain Islam through scientific principles. His established belief that the knowledge of Allah can only be properly shared without any expectation of return has led him to offer all of his works which include books, articles, and videos free of charge via his web-site. In 1970 he started examining the art of spirit evocation and linked these subjects parallel references in the Quran (smokeless flames and flames instilling pores). He found that these references were in fact pointing to luminous energy which led him to write *Spirit, Man, Jinn* while working as a journalist for the Aksam newspaper in Turkey. Published in 1985, his work called '*Mysteries of Man* (*Insan ve Sirlari*)' was Hulusi's first foray into decoding the messages of the Quran filled with metaphors and examples through a scientific backdrop. In 1991 he published *A Guide to Prayer and Dhikr* (*Dua and Zikir*)' where he explains how the repetition of certain prayers and words can lead to the realization of the divine attributes inherent within our essence through increased brain capacity. In 2009 he completed his final work, '*Decoding the Quran, A Unique Sufi Interpretation*' which encompasses the understanding of leading Sufi scholars such as Abdulkarim al Jili, Abdul-Qadir Gilani, Muhyiddin Ibn al-Arabi, Imam Rabbani, Ahmed ar-Rifai, Imam Ghazali, and Razi, and which approached the messages of the Quran through the secret Key of the letter 'B'.

GLOSSARY OF SUFI TERMS

Al-Adl:
The One who provides each of His manifestations their due right in consonance with their creation program. The One who is absolutely free from unjustness or tyranny.

Al-Afuw:
The One who forgives all offences except for 'duality' (*shirq*); the failure to recognize the reality of non-duality prevents the activation of the name *al-Afuw*.

Ahadiyyah:
The absolute oneness of existence.

Ahlul Haqiqah:
The intimates of the reality.

Ahlul Tahqiq:
The people of authenticity.

Al-Akhir:
The infinitely subsequent One, to all creation.

Al-Aleem:
The One who, with the quality of His knowledge, infinitely knows everything in every dimension with all its facets.

Al-Aliy:
The Highest (or the Sublime). The sublime One who observes existence from the point of reality (essence).

Allah:
ALLAH... Such a name... It points to *Uluhiyyah*!

Uluhiyyah encompasses two realities. HU which denotes Absolute Essence (*dhat*) and the realm of infinite points in which every single point is formed by the act of observing knowledge through knowledge.
This act of observing is such that each point signifies an individual composition of Names.

Aql al-Awwal:
The First Intellect; the first disclosure of universal consciousness.

Aql al-Qull:
The Universal Intellect; universal consciousness.

Arsh:
Throne. Denotes universal prolificacy, though not in terms of the perceived material world.

Ashraf al-Mahluq:
The most honored of all creation.

Al-Awwal:	The first and initial state of existence, the essential Name.
Al-Aziz:	The One who, with His unchallengeable might, disposes as He wishes. The One whose will to do as He likes, nothing can oppose. This name works in parallel with the name *Rabb*. The *Rabb* attribute carries out the demands of the Aziz attribute!
Al-Azim:	The magnificent glory beyond any manifestation's capacity of comprehension.
Al-Badee:	The incomparable beauty and the originator of beautiful manifestation! The One who originates innumerable manifestations, all with unique and exclusive qualities, and without any example, pattern, specimen etc.
Al-Baith:	The One who constantly transforms new dimensions of existence.
Al-Basit:	The One who opens and expands; the One who enables dimensional and in-depth sight.
Al-Basir:	The One who is constantly observing His manifestations and evaluating their outputs.
Al-Bari:	The One who fashions all of creation (from micro to macro) with unique functions and designs yet all in conformity with the whole, like the harmonious functioning of all the different organs in the body!
Al-Barr:	The One who eases the actualization of individual temperaments and natural dispositions.
Al-Batin:	The unperceivable reality within the perceivable manifestation! The source of the unknown (*Awwal, Akhir, Zahir, Batin, HU!*)
Al-Baqi:	The Everlasting. The One who exists beyond the concept of time.
Barzakh:	The intermediary dimension.
B-izni-hi (by permission of Allah):	The suitability of the Name composition comprising his essence.
Ad-Darr:	The One who afflicts individuals with various distressing situations (sickness, suffering, trouble) in order to make them turn to Himself!

D'hul Fadhlul Azim:	Possessor of great bounty.
D'hul-Jalali Wal-ikram:	The One who makes individuals experience their 'nothingness' by enabling them to comprehend the reality that they were created from 'naught' and then bestowing them 'Eternity' by allowing them to observe the manifestations of the Names comprising their essence.
Dhu'l Quwwati'l Matin:	Possessor of enduring strength.
Arham-ar-rahimeen:	The One who manifests the infinite qualities of His Names with His grace.
Fath:	Self-conquest.
Al-Fattah:	The One who generates expansion within individuals. The One who enables the recognition and observation of Reality, and hence, that there is no inadequacy, impairment, or mistake in the engendered existence. The One who expands one's vision and activity, and enables their proper usage. The One who enables the recognition and use of the unrecognized (overseen).
Fuad:	Heart - heart neurons. The reflectors of the Names to the brain.
Furqan:	The ability and knowledge to differentiate the right from the wrong or the criterion by which the reality may be differentiated from falsity.
Gabriel:	The disclosure of the knowledge of Allah.
Al-Gaffar:	The One who, as requisites of divine power or wisdom, 'conceals' the inadequacies of those who recognize their shortcomings and wish to be freed from their consequences. The One who forgives.
Al-Ghafur:	The One who's Mercy should never be doubted or given up on. The One who enables necessary cleansing and triggers the name *Rahim* to bestow blessings.
Al-Ghani:	The One who is beyond being labeled and limited by the manifestations of His Names, as He is Great (Akbar) and beyond all concepts. The One who is infinitely abundant with His Names.

Al-Habir:	The One who is aware of the manifestations of His Names at all times. The One who allows his manifestations to discern the level of their comprehension via their outputs.
Al-Hadi:	The guide to the truth. The One who allows individuals to live according to their reality. The articulator of the truth. The guide to reality.
Al-Hafiz:	The One who provides all requirements to preserve and maintain existence.
Al-Hakam:	The Absolute Judge whose judgment (verdict) is irresistibly applied.
Al-Hakim:	The One whose power of knowledge appears under the guise of 'causes', hence creating causality and leading to the perception of multiplicity.
Al-Halim:	The One who refrains from giving sudden (impulsive) reactions to events, but rather evaluates all situations in respect of their purpose of manifestation.
Hamd:	The evaluation of the corporeal worlds created with His Names, as He wills.
Al-Hamid:	The One who observes and evaluates His universal perfection on worldly forms manifested by His Name *al-Waliyy*.
Al-Haqq:	The absolute and unequivocal reality! The source and essence of every function in manifestation!
Al-Hasib:	The One who maintains individuality by holding them to account of their behavioral output through the mechanics of 'consequence'.
Al-Hayy:	The source of names! The One who gives life to the Names and manifests them. The source of universal energy, the essence of energy!
Hu:	Whether via revelation or through consciousness, HU is the inner essence of the reality of everything that is perceived... To such extent that, as the reflection of *Akbariyyah*, first awe then nothingness is experienced and, as such, the Reality of Hu

	can never be attained! Sight cannot reach HU! HU denotes absolute obscurity and incomprehension! As a matter of fact, all names, including Allah are mentioned in connection with HU in the Quran!
Huda:	Guidance; enabling the comprehension of one's essential reality.
Ind'Allah:	From Allah; the forces that are revealed through dimensional emergence to consciousness from the Names of Allah that comprise one's essence.
Insan al-Kamil:	The Perfect Man.
Isra:	The supersensible and dimensional travel by night.
Al-Jabbar:	The One whose will is compelling. The corporeal worlds (engendered existence) are compelled to comply with His demands! There is no room for refusal. This 'jabr' (compelling) quality will inevitably express itself and apply its laws through the essence of beings.
Al-Jalil:	The One who, with His magnificent comprehensiveness and perfection, is the sultan of the world of acts.
Al-Jami:	The One who observes the whole of existence as a multi-dimensional single frame in His Knowledge. The One who gathers creation according to the purpose and function of their creation.
Al-Kabir:	The magnitude of the worlds He created with His Names are incomprehensible.
Kashf al-Nurani:	Enlightened discovery.
Kashf al-Dhulmani:	Purification through suffering.
Al-Karim:	The exceedingly generous and bountiful One who bestows His bounties even upon those who deny His existence. The ability to READ (iqra) is only possible through the activation of this Name, which lies dormant within the essence of every individual.
Al-Khafid:	The One who abases. The One who capacitates a state of existence which is far

from reality. The creator of the *'asfali safileen'* (the lower state of existence). The former of the vision of **'multiplicity'** to conceal the reality.

Al-Khaliq:	The ONE Absolute Creator! The One who brings individuals into the existence from nothingness, with His Names! Everything *al-Khaliq* creates has a purpose to fulfill, and according to this unique purpose, possesses a natural predisposition and character. Hence it has been said:"characterize yourselves with the character of Allah" (Tahallaku biakhlakillah) to mean:Live in accordance with the awareness that you are comprised of the structural qualities of the Names of Allah!
Kitab al-Mubin:	The Clear Book.
Kursi:	Footstool – the actualization and dominance of the reality of the Names.
Ladun:	The potential of the Names comprising one's essence.
Al-Latif:	The One who is subtly present in the depths of every manifestation. The One whose favors are plentiful.
Al-Maalik'ul-Mulk:	The One who governs His Sovereignty as He wishes without having to give account to any individual.
Mahshar:	The place of gathering.
Maiyyah:	Unity of existence.
Al-Majeed:	The One whose majestic glory is evident through His magnificent manifestations!
Al-Majid:	The magnificent and glorious One with unrestricted, infinite generosity and endowment (benevolence).
Mala-i A'la:	The Exalted Assembly.
Al-Maleek:	The Sovereign One, who manifests His Names as he wishes and governs them in the world of acts as He pleases. The one who has providence over all things.
Al-Mani:	The One who prevents those from attaining things they do not deserve!

Manna:	The force of power in the names of Allah comprising your essence.
Marifah:	Gnosis.
Al-Matin:	The One who sustains the world of acts, the steadfast, the creator of robustness and stability, the provider of strength and resistance!
Mawla:	Protector.
Michael:	The force that guides to and enables the attainment of both physical and spiritual sustenance.
Al-Mu'akhkhir:	The One who delays manifestation in consonance with His name *al-Hakim*.
Al-Mubdi:	The One who originates the whole of creation in the corporeal worlds, all with exclusive and unique qualities.
Al-Mudhill:	The One who exposes dishonor in some and degrades below others. The One who deprives from honorable qualities and compels to humiliation with the veil of 'I'ness (ego).
Al-Mughni:	The One who enriches individuals and raises them above others in wealth and emancipates them. The One who enriches with His own riches. The One who grants the beauty of infinity (*baqa*) which results from '*fakr*' (nothingness).
Al-Muhaymin	The One who maintains and protects the manifestations of His Names with His own system. *Al-Muhaymin* also designates the One who safeguards and protects (the trust).
Al-Muhsi:	The creator of the 'forms' (micro to macro) comprising the seeming multiplicities, each equipped with unique qualities and attributes, within UNITY.
Al-Muhyi:	The One who enlivens and enlightens! The One who enables the continuation of the individual's life through the application of knowledge and the observation of one's essential reality.

Al-Mu'id:	The One who restores life to those who turn back to their essence.
Al-Mu'izz:	The Giver of Honor. The One who bestows honor to whom he wishes and holds them in esteem over others.
Al-Mujib:	The One who unequivocally responds to all who turn towards Him (in prayer and invocation) and provides their needs.
Al-Mu'min:	The One who enables the awareness that He, by respect of His Names, is beyond what is perceived. This awareness reflects upon us as **'faith'** (*iman*). All believers, including Rasuls and angels, have their faith rested upon this awareness, which frees the mind from the enslavement of illusion. While illusion can deter the mind, which uses comparison to operate, it becomes powerless and ineffective in the sight of faith. Muqarraboon: Those who have attained the state of divine closeness.
Al-Muntaqim:	The One who makes individuals live the consequences of their actions that impede in the realization of their essence.Al-Mumit: The One who enables a 'taste' (experience)
Al-Mutakabbir:	The One to whom the word 'I' exclusively belongs. Absolute 'I'ness belongs only to Him. Whoever, with the word 'I', accredits a portion of this Absolute 'I'ness to himself, thereby concealing the 'I'ness comprising his essence and fortifying his own relative 'I'ness, will pay its consequence with 'burning' (suffering). Majesty (Absolute 'I'ness) is His attribute alone.
Al-Musawwir:	The fashioner of forms. The One who exhibits 'meanings' as 'forms' and devises the mechanism in the perceiver to perceive them.
Al-Muqeet:	The One who facilitates the expression of the Name *al-Hafiz* by providing the necessary material and spiritual platform for it.
Al-Muqaddim:	The One who expedites (or prioritizes) the manifestation of Names according to their purpose of creation.

Al-Muqsit:	The One who applies justice, as the requirement of His *Uluhiyya*, by endowing every individual their due, based on their unique creation purpose.
Al-Muqtadir:	The Determiner. The absolute possessor of all power pertaining to creation, governance, and disposition.
Al-Muta'ali:	The limitless, boundless Supreme One, whose supremacy encompasses everything! The One whose reality can never be duly reflected by any engendered, conceptualized existence. The One who is beyond being limited by any mind or intellect.
Muttaqeen:	Those who live in line with their essential reality.
An-Nafi:	The One who prompts individuals to engage in good thoughts and actions to aid them towards beneficent and auspicious outcomes.
Nafs:	Self, individual consciousness.

       Nafs-i Ammarah: The Inciting Self.

       Nafs-i Lawwama: The Self-Accusing Self.

       Nafs-i Mulhima: The Inspired Self.

       Nafs-i Mutmainna: The Peaceful Self.

       Nafs-i Radhiya: The Pleased Self.

       Nafs-i Mardhiya: The Pleasing Self.

       Nafs-i Safiya: The Pure Self.

Names:	Divine Names – structural and compositional qualities comprising existence.
Nubuwwah:	The function of enabling people to read and apply the necessary practices of the system of Allah.
An-Nur:	The Knowledge that is the source and essence of everything! The essence of everything is *Nur*; everything is comprised of knowledge. Life subsists with knowledge. Those with knowledge are the ever-living ones (*Hayy*), while those who lack knowledge are like living dead.

Al-Qabid:	The One who exercises His verdict by retaining the essence of an individual's Name reality. The One who restrains and enforces withdrawnness.
Al-Qadir:	The One who creates (discloses, manifests) and observes His knowledge with His power without depending on causality. The One who is absolutely boundless!
Al-Qahhar:	The One who executes the effects of His Name '*Wahid*' and renders invalid the seeming existence of the relative 'I'ness.
Al-Qayyum:	The One who renders Himself existent with His own attributes, without the need of anything. Everything in existence subsists with *al-Qayyum*.
Al-Qawwi:	The One who transforms His power into the enabling potential for the manifestation of existence (hence comprising the force of the whole of existence).
Al-Quddus:	The One who is free and beyond being defined, conditioned and limited by His manifest qualities and concepts! Albeit the engendered existence is the disclosure of His Names, He is pure and beyond from becoming defined and limited by them!
Qurbiyyah:	The state of divine closeness.
Rabb:	The Name composition/divine qualities comprising one's essence.
Ar-Rafi:	The One who exalts. The one who elevates conscious beings to higher states of existence; to enable the realization and observation of their essential reality.
Ar-Rahman:	*Ar-Rahman* signifies the materialization of the essence of every iota with Allah's Names in His knowledge. In modern terms, it designates the quantum potential. It is the potential of the source of the entire creation. It is the name of the Dimension of Names! All things obtain their existence at the level of knowledge and will with the attributes denoted by this name.
Rahmaniyyah:	The quantum potential.

Rahmah:

Ar-Rahim:

Ar-Raqib:

Ar-Rashid:

Rasul:

Al-Ra'uf:

Al-Razzaq:

Rububiyyah:

Ruhu'l Azam:

As-Salam:

As-Sabur:

Samad/Samadiyyah:

Grace.

Ar-Rahim is the Name that brings the infinite qualities of *ar-Rahman* into engendered existence. In this sense, it is the 'observation' of the potential. *Ar-Rahim* observes itself through the forms of existence, by guiding the conscious beings to the awareness that their lives and their essential reality are comprised of and governed by the Names.

The One who watches over and keeps under control the manifestations of His Names, with His names, at all times.

The guider to the right path. The One who allows individuals, who recognize their essential reality, to experience the maturity of this recognition!

One through whom the reality is disclosed - the articulation of Allah's knowledge.

The compassionate and pitying One who protects individuals who turn to Him from all kinds of behavior which may cause harm or trouble to them.

The One who provides all necessary nutrition for the survival of any unit of manifestation regardless of its plane of existence.

Compositional qualities denoted by the Names comprising existence.

The Grand Spirit; the observing One.

A state of emancipation from the conditions

The One who waits for each individual to execute his creation program before rendering effective the consequences of their actions. Allowing the tyranny of the tyrant to take place, i.e. activating the Name *as-Sabur*, is so that both the oppressor and the oppressed can duly carry out their functions before facing the consequences in full effect. Greater calamity forces the creation of increased cruelty.

The Absolutely Self-Sufficient and Whole One.

As-Sami:	The One who perceives His manifestations at every instance. The One who enables awareness and comprehension.
Sayr al-Afaqi:	The recognition of the universal realities.
Sayr al-Anfusi:	The recognition of the individual realities or the path of the inward journey.
Shadid al-Iqab:	Severe in enforcing the due consequence of an offence.
Ash-Shahid:	The One who witnesses His existence through His own existence. The One who observes the disclosure of His Names and witnesses His manifestations!
Ash-Shakur:	The One who allows the proper use of His bestowals in order that He may increase them. The One who enables the due evaluation of resources such that more can be attained. This name triggers the name *al-Karim*.
Shirq:	Duality – the state of assuming the separate existence of an 'other' besides Allah.
Subhan:	One who is beyond being limited or conditioned by any of His manifestations.
Sunnatullah:	The mechanics of the system of Allah.
Tanzih:	The incomparability of the divine.
Taqwa:	Protecting yourself in the way of Allah from the inadequacies of your identity.
Tasbih:	Glorify, exalt – to continue one's existence through Him.
Tashbih:	The similarity/comparability of the divine.
At-Tawwab:	The One who guides individuals to their essence by enabling them to perceive and comprehend the reality. The One who allows individuals to repent, that is, to abandon their misdoings and to compensate for any harm that may have been caused. The activation of this Name triggers the name *Rahim*, and thus benevolence and beauty is experienced.
The Divine Reflections:	
	The Hidden – Reflection of attributes.

	The Secret – Reflection of the Names.
	The Spirit – Fuad: Reflectors of the Names.
	The Heart – Consciousness.
	The Self – Identity – Individual consciousness.
Ubudiyyah:	Servitude of the 'self' or individual consciousness by means of fulfilling its specific function and purpose of creation.
Ulul Albab:	The intimates of the reality through whom Allah hears, sees and speaks.
Al-Wahhab:	The One who bestows and gives unrequitedly to those He wishes, oblivious of deservedness.
Al-Wahid:	The One and only! 'ONE'ness far beyond any concept of multiplicity. The ONE, that isn't composed of (or can be broken into) parts (as in pantheism). The 'ONE'ness that renders duality obsolete! The 'ONE'ness that no mind or intellect can fully comprehend!
Al-Wakil:	The One who provides the means for self-actualization. The One who advocates and protects those who place their trust in Him, providing them with the most auspicious outcomes.
Al-Wali:	The One who governs according to His own verdict.
Wajh:	Divine countenance.
Al-Wasi:	The All-embracing. The One who embraces the whole of existence with the expressions of His Names.
Vicegerent:	Conscious beings who will live with the awareness of the Names.
Al-Wadud:	The creator of attraction. The creator of unconditional and unrequited love. The essence within every beloved!
Al-Wajid:	The One whose qualities and attributes are unfailingly abundant. The manifest One. The One, from which nothing lessens, despite the abundance of His manifestations.

Al-Waliyy:	The One who guides and enables an individual to discover their reality and to live their life in accordance to their essence. It is the source of *risalah* (personification of Allah's knowledge) and *nubuwwah* (prophethood), which comprise the pinnacle states of sainthood (*wilayah*). It is the dispatcher of the perfected qualities comprising the highest point of sainthood, *risalah*, and the state one beneath that, *nubuwwah*.
Waliyy:	Friend, guardian/protector.
Al-Warith:	The One who manifests under various names and forms in order to inherit and protect the possessions of those who abandon all their belongings to undergo true transformation. When one form is exhausted, He continues His existence with another form.
Yakeen:	The state of certainty; to be in complete submission as a result of an absolute comprehension.
	a. The knowledge of certainty (ilm al-yakeen)
	b. The eye of certainty (ayn al-yakeen)
	c. The reality of certainty (haqq al-yakeen)
Az-Zahir:	The self-evident One, the explicit, unequivocal and perceivable manifestation.
Zawj:	While its most common usage is to mean 'partner in marriage' it has also been used in the context of consciousness, implying the partner or equivalent of consciousness.